The Empty Chair

Finding Hope and Joy

Timeless Wisdom from a Hasidic Master,
REBBE NACHMAN OF BRESLOV

Adapted by Moshe Mykoff
and the Breslov Research Institute

For People of All Faiths, All Backgrounds

JEWISH LIGHTS Publishing

Woodstock, Vermont

The Empty Chair: Finding Hope and Joy
Timeless Wisdom from a Hasidic Master, Rebbe Nachman of Breslov

2008 Seventh Printing

Library of Congress Cataloging-in-Publication Data
Mykoff, Moshe.
The empty chair: finding hope & joy: timeless wisdom from a Hasidic master, Rebbe Nachman of Breslov / adapted by Moshe Mykoff and the Breslov Research Institute.
p.   cm.
ISBN-13: 978-1-879045-67-5 (Paperback)
ISBN-10: 1-879045-67-2 (Paperback)
ISBN-10: 1-879045-69-9 (Pb 8-copy display)
1. Joy—Religious aspects—Judaism—Quotations, maxims, etc.
2. Hope—Religious aspects—Judaism—Quotations, maxims, etc.
3. Hasidism—Quotations, maxims, etc.
I. Nahman, of Bratslav, 1772–1811. II. Breslov Research Institute.
III. Title.
BM645.J67M92 1994   94-6763
296.7'2—dc20   CIP

10 9 8 7
Book and cover designed by Glenn Suokko
Printed in Hong Kong

Published by Jewish Lights Publishing
A Division of LongHill Partners, Inc.
Sunset Farm Offices, Route 4, P.O. Box 237
Woodstock, VT 05091
Tel: (802) 457-4000   Fax: (802) 457-4004
www.jewishlights.com

DEDICATION

Rebbe Nachman said: The World has yet to taste what I have to offer. Were they to hear just one of my teachings together with its proper melody and dance, the incredible delight would bring everyone, everything to a state of sheer ecstasy and total transcendence of self.

(Tz #340)

*For all those who've taught me
to fill the empty chair*

— Moshe M.

ACKNOWLEDGMENTS

Translating and adapting this treasure of Rebbe Nachman's aphorisms has been a uniquely fulfilling experience, one which would not have been possible without the help of a special few. I wish to thank two wonderful friends and teachers, Chaim Kramer and Ozer Bergman, whose encouragement and constructive abuse was vital. A word of thanks must also go to Stuart Matlins, my publisher, whose advice and abundant openness made working on this project a true pleasure. Finally, a special thanks to my wife, Elky, whose love and understanding is essential to all that I do.

Moshe Mykoff
Jerusalem, Israel

CONTENTS

THE EMPTY CHAIR

ABOUT THE COVER

The exquisitely hand-crafted chair which appears on the cover belonged to Rebbe Nachman. Tradition has it that it was a gift given to the Rebbe by a follower in 1808. The man, a simple laborer, had worked on it a few hours every day for six months.

During the Cossack uprisings against the Jews of the Ukraine in the early 1920s, the chair was dismantled for safekeeping. In 1936, a family of Breslover Hasidim escaping Europe ahead of the Holocaust brought it to Jerusalem. There, it was reassembled and refurbished by the Israel Museum in 1959, and later restored by Katriel's of Jerusalem.

NOTE ON SOURCES

Each of Rebbe Nachman's aphorisms collected in this book is followed by a reference to where it appears within the corpus of his writings and teachings. These sources appear in abbreviated form, the code for which can be found at the end of the book.

INTRODUCTION

Is the chair you're sitting on empty?

"Ridiculous! How can it be?"

You're right, it can't be... because you're sitting on it.

But it is possible for a person sitting on that chair to feel empty.

Then, the chair is empty—even when occupied!

* * *

Rebbe Nachman of Breslov was about to teach when he suddenly grabbed hold of the chair he was sitting on and said: "When one sits on the chair, one is a *mensch!*"

Webster's defines *mensch* as a person of integrity and honor. For those who know Yiddish it implies more; those familiar with Rebbe Nachman's teachings know it implies even more than that.

In the modern idiom, a *mensch* is a whole human being. It is someone who has integrated the diverse elements of his or her being, both physical and spiritual; someone who has overcome the inner emptiness we sometimes feel. When such a person sits on a chair, the chair is full. One sits on it, and one is a *mensch*.

* * *

Rebbe Nachman of Breslov was born in 1772, in the Ukrainian village of Medzeboz. A great-grandson of Rabbi Israel Baal Shem Tov, founder of the Hasidic movement, Rebbe Nachman attained outstanding levels of saintliness and wisdom. At home in the furthest reaches of Kabbalah mysticism, while at the same time artlessly practical and to-the-point, he taught honesty, simplicity and faith. He wove wondrous tales of princesses, giants, beggars and emperors. He spoke of healing and wholeness... of being alive!

Rebbe Nachman attracted a devoted following, simple folk and scholars alike, who looked to him as "the Rebbe," their prime source of spiritual guidance and support. Even after his passing, in 1810, Rebbe Nachman's influence remained potent. His teachings spread by word of mouth and through his writings. His followers continued to look to his lessons for guidance and inspiration. Today, the movement he initiated is vibrant and growing. Far beyond these circles, Rebbe Nachman's supreme optimism and down-to-earth wisdom have made him one of the most oft-quoted and studied Jewish teachers of all time.

Rebbe Nachman lived at what must count as one of human history's most significant turning-points. His lifetime spanned the beginnings of the Industrial Revolution, the American War of Independence and the French Revolution. Goethe, Kant, Byron, Beethoven and Mozart were all active during the Rebbe's day. In an era poised for a paradigm shift that would engender great reason but also profound doubt, an unparalleled conquering of external frontiers but also an unprecedented inner void, Rebbe Nachman put his finger on the pulse of the dawning age and said: "I'll tell you a secret. Great atheism is coming into the world...."

Almost two hundred years later, don't we know it! We also now know that on the personal level, estrangement from God is paralleled in another form of "great atheism"—an alienation from self.

Addressing an age in which feelings of emptiness would predominate, Rebbe Nachman developed a universal doctrine that speaks to the spiritually seeking as well as to ordinary people facing the problems of everyday living. His message, one of hope and joy, teaches that even where the black-hole-of-self seems most impenetrable, sparks of light are waiting to be released. His words of inspiration reach out to the faithful of any faith, to the not-so-faithful, and even to those with no faith at all.

Outlined in this little treasure of the Rebbe's aphorisms, his prescription for healing and wholeness includes positive thinking, finding good in others and more—all with the aim of *Living in Tune*. To proceed *On the Spiritual Journey* that leads to integration of self, he advocates conscious awareness, binding heart to mind, and empowering oneself with *Faith, Simplicity and Truth*. For *Opening Heaven's Gate* he encourages opening the gates of our hearts, minds and lips through prayer and meditation. All this reaches completion in the way Rebbe Nachman would have us fill the empty chair — the alienated self — by *Leaving Sadness, Finding Hope and Joy*.

1

LIVING IN TUNE

LIVING IN TUNE

For Rebbe Nachman, living in tune meant awareness—being aware of the transient nature of this world and the eternity of the next.

From his window facing the marketplace Rebbe Nachman spotted one of his followers rushing by.

"Have you looked up at the sky this morning?" the Rebbe asked.

"No, Rebbe, I haven't had the time."

"Believe me, in fifty years everything you see here today will be gone. There will be another fair—with other horses, other wagons, different people. I won't be here then and neither will you. So what's so important that you don't have time to look at the sky?!"

Rebbe Nachman of Breslov
taught...

Know! A person walks in life
on a very narrow bridge.
The most important thing
is not to be afraid.

(LM II:48)

Don't make the same mistake
as all those people who give up
trying to change because
they feel stuck in their habits.
If you truly want to, and are
willing to work hard enough,
you can overcome them.

(LM II:110)

Everything in the world—
whatever is and whatever happens
—is a test, designed to give you
freedom of choice. Choose wisely.

(RNW #300)

There's nothing very mysterious
about free will. You do what you
want to do, and you don't do
what you don't want to do.

(LM II:110)

Remember:
Nothing begets wholeness in life
better than a heartfelt sigh.

(LM I:8)

Learn to wait.
If despite all your determined
efforts you cannot seem
to reach your goals, be patient.
Between acceptance and anxiety,
choose acceptance.

(Tz. #431)

All beginnings require that you
unlock new doors.
The key is giving and doing.
Give charity and do kindness.

(LM II:4)

You are
wherever
your thoughts are.

Make sure your thoughts are
where *you* want to be.

(LM I:21)

Is there something you really
want or something you wish
would happen? Focus every ounce
of your concentration on that
thing or event. Visualize it in fine
detail. If your desire is strong
enough and your concentration
intense enough, you can
make it come true.

(RNW #62)

Worldly desires are like sunbeams
in a dark room. They seem solid
until you try to grasp one.

(RNW #6)

Be forewarned:
Man and money
cannot remain together forever.
Either the money is taken
from the man,
or the man is taken
from the money.

(RNW #51)

Money-worship,
like idol-worship, stems from
a lack of trust in God.
The more it is uprooted,
the more the world radiates
with the blessing of the
Holy One's love.

(Ad. p.139)

Become the kind of person who
makes fulfilling physical needs
a spiritual experience.
Some people eat
to have the strength to study
the Word of God.
Others, the more spiritually aware,
study the Word of God
in order to know how to eat.

Whenever possible,
avoid eating in a hurry.
Even at home,
don't gobble up your food.
Eating is an act of holiness.
It requires full presence of mind.

(Tz. #515)

When you feel yourself getting angry,
stop.
Imagine yourself
as having already exploded and
you now feel wasted. For that's
what happens when you get angry:
your soul leaves you.
Do this, and your anger
is sure to dissolve.

(LM I:68)

Answer insult with silence.
When someone hurts you,
do not answer in kind. You will
then be worthy of genuine honor
—honor that is inner honor,
honor from Above.

(LM I:6)

Peace heals.

When your own world
is fractured, increase your
knowledge of God. It will
spawn inner peace.

When the outside world
is fractured, promote the
search for truth. It will
spawn universal peace.

(LM I:27)

The highest peace is the peace
between opposites.

(LM I:80)

If you remember this the next
time you meet someone who
makes you uncomfortable,
instead of heading for the nearest
exit, you'll find ways for the two
of you to get along.

(Ad. p.258)

Be like God and don't look for
people's shortcomings and
weak points. You will then be at
peace with everyone.

(Ad. p.258)

It's easy to criticize others and
make them feel unwanted.
Anyone can do it.
What takes effort and skill is
picking them up and
making them feel good.

(NT #31)

Always look for the good
in the other.

Focus on that good, highlight it,
and turn even sinner into saint.

(LM I:282)

Always look for the good
in yourself.

Focus on that good,
highlight it, and turn even
depression into joy.

(LM I:282)

When asked how things are,
don't whine and grumble about
your hardships. If you answer
"Lousy," then God says,
"You call this bad? I'll show you
what bad really is!"

When asked how things are and,
despite hardship or suffering,
you answer
"Good," then God says,
"You call this good? I'll show you
what good really is!"

(NT #46)

The Architect of the world
never does the same thing twice.
Every day is an entirely
new creation. Take as much as
you can from what each new
day has to offer.

(LH 1:123d)

Work on having only positive
thoughts. It will do wonders
for your mind.

(LM I:21)

Each day has its own set of
thoughts, words and deeds.
Live in tune.

(LM I:54)

2

ON THE SPIRITUAL
JOURNEY

ON THE SPIRITUAL JOURNEY

Rebbe Nachman said that, often, even just his daily religious obligations felt like a crushing burden. But the Rebbe found a way to bear the weight of his devotions by each morning saying to himself, "I will ignore tomorrow and all future tomorrows—today is all there is!"

The Rebbe understood that what wears us down most on our spiritual journey is the feeling that there is too much to accomplish. Instead, he advised focusing only on the task at hand. By doing so, we can overcome even the most daunting obstacles.

Spiritual awakening begins with
inspiration coming from Without.
Then, once you are already on the
road, the real work begins.
Keep at it and inspiration will
come from within.

(LH 3:152c)

In the early stages of your
spiritual journey, it may seem that
Heaven is rejecting you and
spurning all your efforts.
Stay on course. Don't give up.
In time, all barriers will disappear.

(LM II:48)

Growing spiritually can be like
a roller coaster ride. Take comfort
in the knowledge that
the way down is only
preparation for the way up.

(LM I:22)

Go carefully:
Spiritual growth must proceed
slowly and steadily.
Too often we want to improve
ourselves and our relationships so
quickly that we make ourselves
frustrated and confused.

(RNW #27)

Never insist that everything
go exactly your way,
even in matters spiritual.

(Tz. #433)

Believe that none of the effort
you put into coming closer to God
is ever wasted—even if in the
end you don't achieve what
you are striving for.

(RNW #12)

Be strong-willed and stubborn
if you want to get closer to God.
How else will you survive all
the difficulties that are sure
to come your way?

(LM I:22)

Don't be frustrated by
the obstacles you encounter on your
spiritual journey. They are there
by design, to increase your desire
for the goal you seek.
Because the greater your goal,
the greater the yearning you'll
need to achieve it.

(LM I:66)

Always remember:
You are never given an obstacle
you cannot overcome.

(LM II:46)

Sometimes a particular devotion
seems ideal for getting close
to God. Later, a different devotion
seems better.
Why confuse yourself?
Whatever you do is good,
as long as you do no wrong.

(RNW #269)

Occupy yourself with doing good,
and the bad will automatically
fall away.

(RNW #12)

The most direct means for
attaching ourselves to God from
this material world is through
music and song.

Even if you can't sing well, sing.
Sing to yourself. Sing in the
privacy of your own home.
But sing.

(RNW #273)

Never miss an opportunity to
study the Word of God. It settles
the mind and calms the heart.

(Ad. p.269)

God's Word is the source of all
true life. Know and understand it.
The Word can heal your soul and
unite it with its source.

(LM I:74)

Sanctify your mouth through
prayer and study; your nostrils
through the long breath of
patience;
your ears by listening
to the words of the wise;
and your eyes by
shutting them to evil.

(LM I:21)

It is not enough to know God
only in the mind.
Bind understanding to your
heart so that the awe of
The Holy One's greatness results in
true devotion.

(Ad. p.60)

Fill your heart with desire and
yearning for God. Long to serve
The Holy One properly.
For in practice, considering God's
greatness, no human service is
ever adequate. Just do the
best you can.

(Tz. #554, RNW #51)

Make every effort to increase
your longing for God. Of course,
this alone is not enough;
it must be realized in action.
But even if you are not worthy of
achieving your spiritual goals,
the yearning is still very precious
and deserves reward.

(RNW #260)

Never succumb to feelings
of loneliness. No matter where
you are, God is close by.

Remember:
Feeling distant from God
is subjective, not objective;
it is just your own feeling,
not reality.

(RNW #52)

The light of the Infinite One is
without form and only takes
shape — for good or bad — in the
recipient. Therefore it is up to us.
We have to do our best to shape
God's light into blessing,
not curse.

(LM I:3)

THE EMPTY CHAIR

Take care, there is much power
in a glance. If accompanied by a
malicious thought, it can cause harm.
This is what is known
as the evil eye.

(RNW #27)

Have a good eye. Always see good
in others. Spiritual awareness
depends upon it.
Spiritual awareness is lost when people
dull their hearts with jealousy and
develop an evil eye.

(LM I:54)

Seek the sacred within the
ordinary. Seek the remarkable
within the commonplace.

Is not the Song of Songs at once
a love song and the holiest of
all sacred teachings?

(LM I:243)

Abandon all worldly concern
in your spiritual quest and you'll
be called a fanatic. But, do not
consider devotion to God
fanaticism. If anything, it is those
who devote themselves to
worldly pleasures who are the
real fanatics.

Even what the world considers
fanaticism is unnecessary.
It is possible to get close to God
without abandoning everything.

(RNW #51)

Thirsting for God
is our task
in this world.

Quenching that thirst
will be our reward
in the World to Come.

(RNW #259)

3

...WITH FAITH,
SIMPLICITY AND TRUTH

...WITH FAITH, SIMPLICITY AND TRUTH

Rebbe Nachman taught: The search for truth, about our world and our selves, must be vigorously pursued. We must be as honest as we are resolute. And when our search is accompanied by faith and simplicity, we have no lingering doubts or paralyzing impasses— only joyous contentment.

People consider faith a minor
thing. But I consider it very,
very important.

(RNW #33)

Do all you can to develop
your faith in God.

Faith is the foundation of all
spiritual quest...the root of all
teaching and practice...
the channel for every benefit
and blessing.

(RNW #261)

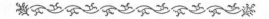

For the true believer,
believing is seeing.

(Ad. p.11)

Better to be a fool who believes
everything than a skeptic
who believes nothing—
not even the truth.

(RNW #103)

Use every means to build your
faith. This includes finding ways
to build solid faith in a righteous
teacher...and in yourself.

(RNW #141)

Affirm your faith in yourself:

~ I believe that I am very
   important in God's eyes.

~ I believe that I can return,
   no matter how far I've strayed.

~ I believe that I have the
   inner strength to change.

~ I believe that I can become truly
   devoted and close to God.

Faith makes you truly alive.
It fills your every day with good.
When troubles come, as they will,
take comfort in your faith that
whatever happens is for the best.

(RNW #32)

Take note:
Everything can be a resource for
serving God. But the more faith
is lacking, the more people turn to
laborious and complex devotions.

(LM II:86)

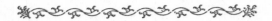

Steer clear of sophistication and
cleverness; they add nothing
to coming closer to God.
All you need is simplicity,
sincerity and faith.

After all, isn't God higher than
all else? Yet isn't God also
profoundly simple?

(RNW #101)

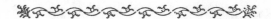

Rely on nothing and no one but God. This is true simplicity. Anything else means pursuing a complicated course of action.

(Ad. p.247)

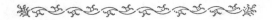

Did you ever notice that
the further people are from truth,
the more they consider someone
who turns away from evil
to be a fool?

When there is no truth in the
world, anyone who wants to turn
away from evil has no choice
but to play the fool.

(ABB p.9)

Human fallibility being what it is,
victory and truth
do not always go together. Therefore,
if you have to always win,
you can't always be true.

(LM I:122)

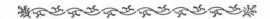

Truth is one. Falsehood is many.

Falsehood causes the mind's eye
to see double, so what is one
looks like two, and what is whole
looks divided. Always strive for
the "perfect vision" of truth.

(LM I:51)

Develop a good eye.
Always looking for good
will bring you to truth.

Even with a good eye, be careful
not to rush judgment. This is no
different than looking at
something from afar and drawing
the wrong conclusion.

(LM I:51)

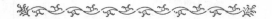

To be a person of truth,
be swayed neither by approval
nor disapproval.

Work at not needing approval
from anyone and you will be free
to be who you really are.

(LM I:66)

Truth is the "light" by which
to find your way out of darkness.
Turn it on.

(LM I:9)

4

OPENING HEAVEN'S GATE

OPENING HEAVEN'S GATE

Rebbe Nachman suggested a number of ways for opening Heaven's gate, including: standard and spontaneous prayer; *hitbodedut,* his unique form of meditation; and the silent scream.

The Rebbe said: When do I have my meditation? When everyone is around me, that's when I seclude myself with God. I know how to cry out in a silent scream. What I say is heard from one end of the world to the other, yet those around me hear nothing!

Anyone can do this. Imagine the sound of such a scream in your mind. Just as the throat brings sound from your lungs to your lips, there are nerves that draw sound into your head. When you do this, you are shouting inside your brain. Direct that shout to the One above and it will open Heaven's gate.

Pray. Pray. Pray.
Whatever you need...praying is
the best way to get it.

(RNW #233)

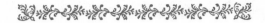

Pray with emotion,
and God will forgive you.

(ABB p.237)

Pray with an attentive heart,
and see all of heaven's doors
open before you.

(ABB p.70)

Pray with joy, and watch your
requests ascend straight
to God's chamber.

(ABB p.245)

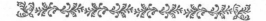

Go out and defeat God.
Yes, God actually wants us to
conquer, wants us to keep praying
and praying until we "force"
the Holy One to forgive us for
what we've done.

(RNW #69)

As often as you can, take a trip
out to the fields to pray.
All the grasses will join you.
They will enter your prayers
and give you strength to sing
praises to God.

(LM II:11)

Praise God. It puts everything into
its proper place and perspective.

(LM I:27)

Keep in mind
that the essence of your prayers is
the faith you have in them
that they will be answered.

(LM I:7)

While praying, listen to the
words very carefully. When your
heart is attentive, your entire
being enters your prayer without
your having to force it.

(RNW #66)

How very good it is when you
can awaken your heart and plead
to God until tears stream from
your eyes, and you stand like
a little child crying to its parent.

(RNW #7)

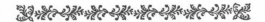

Speech has a great power to
awaken a person spiritually.

Address God in your own words.
Compose your own prayers.
Doing this will draw forth
your soul and stir your
meditative faculties.

(LM II:98)

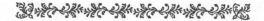

Hitbodidut-meditation—
inner-directed, unstructured,
active self-expression
before God—
is the highest path of all.
Take it.

(LM II:25)

Make it a daily habit to seclude
yourself in *hitbodidut*-meditation.
Express your innermost thoughts
and feelings before God each day
in the language you are most
comfortable with.

(LM II:96)

Talk to God as you would talk
to your very best friend.
Tell The Holy One everything.

(LM II:99)

Even if all you can say to God is
"Help!" it is still very good.
Repeat this over and over again,
until God opens your lips and
the words begin to flow
from your heart.

(LM II:96)

And even when no words come,
do not despair. Come back day
after day to your secluded spot
and wait. Just wanting to speak to
God is in itself a very great thing.

(LM II:25)

The height
of *hitbodidut*-meditation
is when, because of
your great longing to unite with
God, you feel your soul bound to
your body by no more than a
single strand. Is there anything
better to strive for in this life?

(LM II:99)

Most of all, prayer is the gate
through which we enter to God.
Learn to pray and you'll come
to know and be attached to
The Holy One.

(LM II:94)

5

LEAVING SADNESS, FINDING HOPE & JOY

LEAVING SADNESS, FINDING HOPE & JOY

Rebbe Nachman was shattered, empty. His infant son had just died. Although the Rebbe's closest followers had come to console him, they could not bear to witness his torment and ran from the room.

When they returned the next day, the Rebbe said to them, "Had you not run out, I would have told you something beautiful." He then taught a lesson entitled Garden of the Souls, explaining how we can extract meaning from even our greatest suffering. This is what we must do if we are to leave sadness and find hope and joy.

Always remember:
Joy is not merely incidental to
your spiritual quest.
It is vital.

(LM I:24)

Nothing is as liberating as joy.
It frees the mind and fills it
with tranquillity.

(LM II:10)

Losing hope
is like losing your freedom,
like losing your self.

(Ad. p.253)

Finding true joy is the hardest of
all spiritual tasks. If the only way
to make yourself happy
is by doing something silly,
do it.

(Ad. p.254)

Depression
does tremendous damage.
Use every ploy you can think of
to bring yourself to joy.

(LM II:48)

Today you feel up.
Don't let yesterdays and
tomorrows bring you down.

(RNW #288)

If despite your desire to be happy
you feel down, draw strength
from happier times gone by.
Eventually, joy will return.

(LM I:222)

If you don't feel happy,
pretend to be.
Even if you are downright depressed,
put on a smile. Act happy.
Genuine joy will follow.

(RNW #74)

Get into the habit of singing
a tune. It will give you
new life and fill you with joy.

(Ad. p.188)

Get into the habit of dancing.
It will displace depression and
dispel hardship.

(LM I:41)

Always wear a smile.
The gift of life will then be
yours to give.

Sometimes, people are terribly
distressed but have no one to
whom they can unburden
themselves. If you come along
with a happy face, you cheer them
and give them new life.

(RNW #43)

Don't confuse heartbreak with
sadness and depression.
Depression is really anger, a
complaint against God for not
giving you what you want.
But when you have a contrite
heart you are like a little child
crying because its parent
is far away.

(RNW #41,42)

When you're happy,
it's easy to set aside some time
to pray with a contrite heart.
But when you're depressed,
secluding yourself to speak with God
is very hard to do.

That's why being happy
is so important that you should even
force yourself to be happy,
if that's what it takes.

(RNW #20)

Most people think of
forgetfulness as a defect.
I consider it a great benefit.

Being able to forget frees you
from the burdens of the past.

(RNW #25)

Avoid depression at all cost.
It is the root of all illness
and dis-ease.

(LM II:24)

THE EMPTY CHAIR

Never despair! Never!
It is forbidden to give up hope.

(LM II:78)

No matter how far you've
strayed, returning to God is
always possible.
Agree therefore that there is
absolutely no place for despair.

(RNW #3)

Never despair of crying out,
praying and pleading with God.
Keep at it until you succeed;
until the Nearness you long for
is yours.

(Tz. #565)

If you believe that you can
damage, then believe that
you can fix.

If you believe that you can harm,
then believe that you can heal.

(LM II:112)

Remember:
Things can go from the very worst
to the very best...
...in just the blink of an eye.

SOURCES

Abbreviations:

Ad.   *Advice,* Breslov Research Institute,
        1983
AB   *Avaneha Barzel,* Chasidei Breslov
ABB   *The Aleph-Bet Book,* Breslov
        Research Institute, 1986
LH   *Likutey Halakhot,* Vols. 1–8,
        Chasidei Breslov
LM   *Likutey Moharan,* Vols. I and II,
        Chasidei Breslov
NT   *N'tiv Tzaddik,* Chasidei Breslov
Tz.   *Tzaddik,* Breslov Research Institute,
        1987
RNW   *Rabbi Nachman's Wisdom,*
        Breslov Research Institute, 1973

ABOUT THE BRESLOV RESEARCH INSTITUTE

Rebbe Nachman was only 38 years old when he passed away in 1810. Yet, shortly before his passing, he told his followers that his influence would endure long afterwards. "My light will burn until the days of the Mashiach [Messiah]." Generations of readers have been enthralled and inspired by his writings, which have been explored and interpreted by leading scholars around the globe.

The growing interest in Rebbe Nachman from all sectors—academia and laymen alike — led to the establishment of the Breslov Research Institute in Jerusalem in 1979. Since then a team of scholars has been engaged in research into the texts, oral traditions and music of the Breslov movement. The purpose of the Institute is to publish authoritative translations, commentaries and general works on Breslov Chassidut. Projects also include the recording of Breslov songs and melodies on cassettes and in music book form.

Offices and representatives of the Breslov
Research Institute:

Israel:

Breslov Research Institute
P.O. Box 5370
Jerusalem, Israel
Tel: (011-9722) 582-4641
Fax: (011-9722) 582-5542
www.breslov.org

North America:

Breslov Research Institute
P.O. Box 587
Monsey, NY 10952-0587
Tel: (845) 425-4258
Fax: (845) 425-3018
www.breslov.org

Breslov books may be ordered directly from
these offices or from Jewish Lights Publishing.
Ordering information is provided at the end
of this book.

ABOUT JEWISH LIGHTS PUBLISHING

People of all faiths and backgrounds yearn for books that attract, engage, educate and spiritually inspire.

Our principal goal is to stimulate thought and help all people learn about who the Jewish People are, where they come from, and what the future can be made to hold. While people of our diverse Jewish heritage are the primary audience, our books speak to people in the Christian world as well and will broaden their understanding of Judaism and the roots of their own faith.

We bring to you authors who are at the forefront of spiritual thought and experience. While each has something different to say, they all say it in a voice that you can hear. Our books are designed to welcome you and then to engage, stimulate and inspire. We judge our success not only by whether or not our books are beautiful and commercially successful, but by whether or not they make a difference in your life.

Spiritual Inspiration

THESE ARE THE WORDS
A Vocabulary of Jewish Spiritual Life
by *Arthur Green*
6 x 9, 304 pp, PB, 978-1-58023-107-7 **$18.95**

THE ENNEGRAM AND
KABBALAH, 2ND ED.
Reading Your Soul
by *Rabbi Howard A. Addison*
6 x 9, 192 pp, PB, 978-1-58023-229-6 **$16.99**

GOD'S TO-DO LIST
103 Ways to Be an Angel
and Do God's Work on Earth
by *Dr. Ron Wolfson*
6 x 9, 144 pp, PB, 978-1-58023-301-9 **$15.99**

SACRED INTENTIONS
Daily Inspiration to Strengthen the Spirit,
Based on Jewish Wisdom
by *Rabbi Kerry M. Olitzky* and
Rabbi Lori Forman
4½ x 6½, 448 pp, PB, 978-1-58023-061-2 **$15.95**

FILLING WORDS WITH LIGHT
Hasidic and Mystical Reflections
on Jewish Prayer
by *Lawrence Kushner* and *Nehemia Polen*
5½ x 8½, 176 pp, PB, 978-1-58023-238-8 **$16.99**

Spiritual Inspiration for Family Life

TOUGH QUESTIONS JEWS ASK *For ages 12 & up*
**A Young Adult's Guide to
Building a Jewish Life**
by *Rabbi Edward Feinstein*
6 x 9, 160 pp, PB, 978-1-58023-139-8 **$14.99**

THE KIDS' FUN BOOK OF JEWISH TIME
by *Emily Sper*
9 x 7½, 24 pp, Full-color illus., HC, 978-1-58023-311-8 **$16.99**

**FOR KIDS—PUTTING GOD ON
YOUR GUEST LIST, 2ND ED.**
**How to Claim the Spiritual Meaning of
Your Bar or Bat Mitzvah**
by *Rabbi Jeffrey K. Salkin*
6 x 9, 144 pp, PB, 978-1-58023-308-8 **$15.99**

For ages 9 & up   **THE BOOK OF MIRACLES**
**A Young Person's Guide
to Jewish Spiritual Awareness**
by *Rabbi Lawrence Kushner*
6 x 9, 96 pp, HC, Two-color illustrations. 978-1-879045-78-1 **$16.95**

WHEN A GRANDPARENT DIES
**A Kid's Own Remembering Workbook for
Dealing with Shiva and the Year Beyond**
by *Nechama Liss-Levinson, PhD*
8 x 10, 48 pp, HC, Two-color text. 978-1-879045-44-6 **$15.95**
For ages 7–13

Add Greater Meaning to Your Life

THE WOMEN'S TORAH COMMENTARY
New Insights from Women Rabbis
on the 54 Weekly Torah Portions
Edited by *Rabbi Elyse Goldstein*
6 x 9, 496 pp, HC, 978-1-58023-076-6 **$34.95**

THE WOMEN'S
HAFTARAH COMMENTARY
New Insights from Women Rabbis on the 54
Weekly Haftarah Portions,
the 5 Megillot & Special Shabbatot
Edited by *Rabbi Elyse Goldstein*
6 x 9, 560 pp, HC, 978-1-58023-133-6 **$39.99**

THE WAY INTO THE
VARIETIES OF JEWISHNESS
by *Sylvia Barack Fishman, PhD*
6 x 9, 288 pp, HC, 978-1-58023-030-8 **$24.99**

A DREAM OF ZION
American Jews Reflect on
Why Israel Matters to Them
Edited by *Rabbi Jeffrey K. Salkin*
6 x 9, 304 pp, HC, 978-1-58023-340-8 **$24.99**